Jazz Phrasing for Saxophone
Volume 2

by Greg Fishman

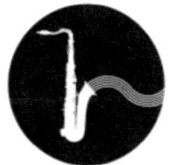

Published by Greg Fishman Jazz Studios
Evanston, Illinois 60202

ISBN: 978-0-9843492-2-7

©2010 Greg Fishman

All rights reserved. International copyright secured. No part of this book or CD set may be reproduced or transmitted in any form or by any means, electronic or mechanical, including photocopying or recording, or by any information storage and retrieval system, without permission in writing from the publisher. Violation of copyright is subject to all applicable laws.

Published by Greg Fishman Jazz Studios
824 Custer Avenue, Evanston, Illinois 60202
www.gregfishmanjazzstudios.com

Jazz Phrasing for Saxophone
Volume 2

Table of Contents

Preface…………………………………………………………………....	4
Credits……………………………………………………………………...	5
Suggested Use of This Book and CD Set………………………….	6
Style and Analysis……………………………………………………...	9
Detailed Overview of the Songs……………………………………..	11
Castlewood Terrace …………………………………………………...	12
Garfield Boulevard……………………………………………………..	14
Dayton Street……………………………………………………………	16
Hyde Park Boulevard………………………………………………….	18
Pulaski Road……………………………………………………………	20
Orchard Street………………………………………………………….	22
Fargo Avenue…………………………………………………………..	24
School Street…………………………………………………………..	26
Lexington Avenue……………………………………………………..	28
Edgewater Avenue…………………………………………………….	30
Thematic Index..	32
About the Author……………………………………………………....	36

©2010 Greg Fishman
All rights reserved. International copyright secured.

PREFACE

Applying good phrasing to music is like using good punctuation in written or spoken language. It involves the grouping of ideas to make the meaning of the words clear to the listener. The words are grouped into sentences, and the sentences are then grouped into paragraphs. The same is true when interpreting a piece of music. Good phrasing requires a musician to interpret the notes he plays, and determine which notes need to be grouped together to form a complete musical idea.

Throughout this book, each song is designed to train your ear to hear the logical grouping of phrases through the use of sequence and thematic development.

While the art of good phrasing involves the interpretation of note groupings and their relationships, it also involves deciding where you're going to take a breath. Read the following sentences aloud to compare examples of good and bad phrasing.

Good phrasing, spoken in one continuous breath:

"Ladies and gentlemen, it gives me great pleasure to introduce the senior class president."

Bad phrasing, spoken with extra breaths, disrupting the flow and grouping of the words:

"Ladies and gentlemen, it gives (breath) me great pleasure to introduce the senior class (breath) president."

The difference between these two sentences is very similar to the difference between a professional musician's phrasing and a student's phrasing. Both may be playing the correct notes with the correct rhythm, but the professional musician knows how to group the notes in a smooth, flowing fashion, while the student takes breaths at random, not even aware that he's disrupting the phrasing.

Jazz Phrasing for Saxophone has been carefully designed to help you learn to phrase like a professional player.

These are pieces that will be fun for all musicians who love melodic writing with good thematic development. I hope that you get many years of enjoyment from this book.

— Greg Fishman

If you'd like to play through the entire book using only the sax demonstration tracks, simply program your CD player to play the odd-numbered tracks only (1,3,5,7, etc.).

If you'd like to play through the entire book with just the rhythm section tracks, program your CD player to play the even-numbered tracks only (2,4,6,8, etc.).

If you need a tuning note, play track 21.

Use the odd-numbered CD tracks to familiarize yourself with the phrasing, articulation, and general feel of each piece. Play along with these tracks and match the phrasing, time feel and articulation.

Once you're comfortable playing along with the recorded demonstration and rhythm section tracks, experiment with playing some chord tones or voice-leading lines along with the play-along CD. This is a great way to train your ear.

TEMPOS

The pieces in this book focus primarily on medium tempos, and each piece was written to be played at the tempo marked. However, if you feel that you can't yet keep up with the recorded tempo, set your metronome at half the marked tempo and play through the piece. Circle any passage that poses a technical challenge, and practice the circled areas until you can play them smoothly and accurately. The final "test" for any tempo is whether or not you can successfully play the entire piece in time, with the correct style and articulation, with no mistakes. Once you've achieved this goal, you're ready to turn the metronome one click faster and continue repeating this process until you've reached the marked tempo.

DYNAMICS

A suggested dynamic level is marked at the beginning of each song. However, within each piece, and each phrase, there are often what I call "micro-dynamics." These are subtle differences between the weighting of notes in a phrase, and these have a dramatic effect on the phrasing and feel of the piece. If you listen carefully to the recording, you can hear me making these dynamic choices, too subtle and numerous to notate, but there for you to hear and study, nonetheless.

Think of these micro-dynamics as you would think of small waves of water on a smooth lake. The lake is calm, but there's still some movement in the water, as opposed to a pail of water with no motion whatsoever.

I encourage you to experiment with different dynamics on the pieces, and, as a general rule, start the pieces at a comfortably moderate dynamic level so that you leave yourself some room to build the dynamic level for the repeat of the piece.

ARTICULATION

Crisp, clear articulation in music is the equivalent of good diction used in any spoken language. Throughout this book I have included articulation markings to convey the basic style of each piece. However, I recommend repeated listenings to the play-along CDs, which will reveal more subtle nuances of articulation.

THEMATIC INDEX

Turn to page thirty-two of this book to see a thematic index of all ten songs. This index provides an easy to use, "at-a-glance" look at the opening theme of each song. Use the thematic index to compare the different opening themes of the songs, as well as a way to select the piece you'd like to play, based on the key signature, tempo, starting interval or song style.

The opening interval of each theme, as well as the direction of the interval (ascending or descending) is also listed on the index. This will be useful for ear-training purposes. For example, the opening interval of "Fargo Avenue" is an ascending minor third. Memorizing the sound of the first two notes of this song will help you to remember the sound of an ascending minor third.

In addition to recognizing the opening interval, it's also important to hear the interval in its proper harmonic context. For example, both "Dayton Street " and "Hyde Park Boulevard" open with a descending major third, but the interval acts as the seventh and fifth of the first chord of "Dayton Street," while on "Hyde Park Boulevard," the major third interval acts as the third and the root of the song's first chord.

Every note has a unique flavor, depending on its harmonic context. For example, a "C" played as the root of a Cma7 chord sounds different than that same "C" as the third of an Ab7 chord. Whenever you play a song, try to hear the melody notes as they relate to the underlying chords.

MORE RESOURCES AVAILABLE ONLINE

If you'd like to read more about my concepts on jazz improvisation, please go to my educational website: www.gregfishmanjazzstudios.com. There are downloadable articles on theory and ear-training, as well as a variety of licks and useful practice tips.

PRIVATE LESSONS

Private lessons include the study of improvisation, transcription, ear-training, jazz vocabulary, playing in twelve keys, articulation, thematic development, memorization techniques and music theory. All playing levels are welcome. To schedule a private lesson in person or via webcam, please contact me at (847)334-3634 or greg@gregfishmanjazzstudios.com.

STYLE & ANALYSIS

SEQUENCES

Sequences make a song sound more structured and melodic. They involve the use of repeated melodic, rhythmic or harmonic patterns. The pitches of the repeated pattern are often transposed to fit a new harmonic setting.

Sequences usually occur in groups of two, three or four, with the original idea serving as the "model" sequence upon which subsequent sequences are based. The challenge for a composer or improvisor using sequences is knowing how many times to repeat an idea. If there are too few sequences, the song won't sound catchy, yet, if you have too many sequences, the song gets too predictable. When you have the right number of sequences, a song sounds melodically balanced.

Play the following example and notice the way in which sequence is used to give the song a "catchy" sound:

"Hyde Park Boulevard," mm.1-8

In the example above, the opening theme (labeled as the model) is sequenced three times, for a total of four statements of the original melodic idea.

There are two different types of sequences; direct and indirect. When a theme is repeated immediately after the model, as in measures one through four in the example above, it is called a "direct sequence."

If there is new melodic material before the restatement of the model, it is called an "indirect sequence." Measures five through eight in the example above would be considered an inderect sequece becuase of the new melodic material which occurs in the sixth measure.

As an experiment to demonstrate the importance and power of sequence, play the example above, and stop playing at the end of the sixth measure. Your ear will hear that the model idea hasn't been repeated enough times, and you'll feel as though the musical thought stopped in mid-sentence.

Next, play the excerpt above once more, but as originally written, playing through the end of the eighth measure. When you hear the third sequence of the theme in the seventh measure, you'll hear that the phrase is now balanced and complete. If you want to hear some truly amazing sequences, listen to any music by J.S. Bach, one of my all-time musical heroes.

VARIATION

While sequence is used to restate a theme, often transposing the idea to fit into a new harmonic context, variation is used to elaborate on the theme through the use of additional notes and changes to the rhythms used in the original theme.

Play the variation used in "Dayton Street" below:

"Dayton Street," mm.7-8

"Dayton Street," mm.23-24

Notice how the original theme has been expanded, keeping the original minor third interval used in measure seven, but adding new notes and changing the rhythm to expand the original one-measure idea into a two-measure phrase.

VOICE-LEADING

Voice-leading is the act of smoothly connecting notes from one chord to another, while moving a distance of no more than a whole-step (ascending or descending). Note the use of voiceleading in this example from "School Street" below:

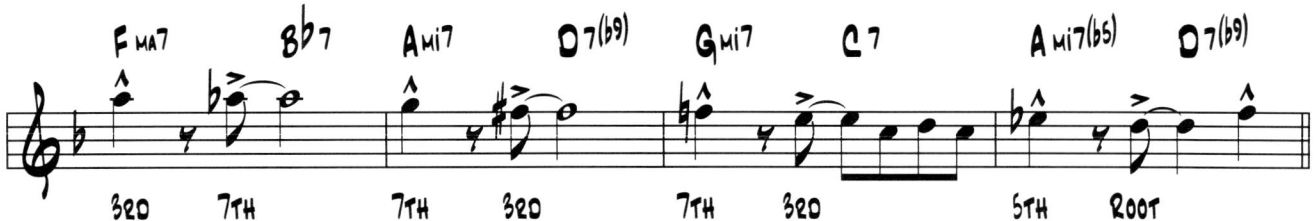

"School Street," mm.1-4

The excerpt above is a good example of effective voiceleading because it highlights the sound the current chord changing to a new chord with a minimum of movement.

As you learn to recognize the sound of voice-leading, you'll start to notice some common patterns such as those used above. The most common (and one of the most useful) of all voice-leading patterns is the "3rd to 7th" and "7th to 3rd" pattern, often used when chords move in the circle of fourths, as in the "School Street" example above.

DETAILED OVERVIEW OF THE SONGS

Title	Tempo	Style	Form	Length of Form	Saxophone Key Signature	Page Number	CD Track Numbers
Castlewood Terrace	♩ = 112	Swing	AABA	32 Bars	D Major	12	1. & 2.
Garfield Boulevard	♩ = 140	Swing	ABAC	32 Bars	A Minor	14	3. & 4.
Dayton Street	♩ = 192	Samba	AABA	56 Bars	A Major	16	5. & 6.
Hyde Park Boulevard	♩ = 160	Swing	AABA	32 Bars	G Major	18	7. & 8.
Pulaski Road	♩ = 126	Swing	BLUES	12 Bars	C Major	20	9. & 10.
Orchard Street	♩ = 168	Bossa	ABAB	40 Bars	G Major	22	11. & 12.
Fargo Avenue	♩ = 86	Ballad	AABA	32 Bars	C Major	24	13. & 14.
School Street	♩ = 132	Shuffle	AABA	32 Bars	F Major	26	15. & 16.
Lexington Avenue	♩ = 144	Swing	AABA	32 Bars	D Major	28	17. & 18.
Edgewater Avenue	♩ = 196	Swing	AABA	32 Bars	G Major	30	19. & 20.

CD TRACK #1 (SAXOPHONE + RHYTHM SECTION)
CD TRACK #2 (RHYTHM SECTION ONLY)

COUNT OFF: 2 BARS (6 CLICKS)

GREG FISHMAN

Castlewood Terrace

CD TRACK #3 (SAXOPHONE + RHYTHM SECTION)
CD TRACK #4 (RHYTHM SECTION ONLY)

COUNT OFF: 2 BARS (6 CLICKS)

Greg Fishman

Garfield Boulevard

©2010 Greg Fishman Jazz Studios
All Rights Reserved. Copyright Secured.

CD TRACK #5 (SAXOPHONE + RHYTHM SECTION)
CD TRACK #6 (RHYTHM SECTION ONLY)

COUNT OFF: 2 BARS (6 CLICKS)

Dayton Street

Greg Fishman

CD TRACK #7 (SAXOPHONE + RHYTHM SECTION)
CD TRACK #8 (RHYTHM SECTION ONLY)

COUNT OFF: 2 BARS (6 CLICKS)

Greg Fishman

Hyde Park Boulevard

©2010 Greg Fishman Jazz Studios
All Rights Reserved. Copyright Secured.

CD TRACK #9 (SAXOPHONE + RHYTHM SECTION)
CD TRACK #10 (RHYTHM SECTION ONLY)

COUNT OFF: 2 BARS (6 CLICKS)

Greg Fishman

Pulaski Road

CD TRACK #13 (SAXOPHONE + RHYTHM SECTION)
CD TRACK #14 (RHYTHM SECTION ONLY)

COUNT OFF: 1 BAR (4 CLICKS)

Greg Fishman

Fargo Avenue

CD TRACK #15 (SAXOPHONE + RHYTHM SECTION)
CD TRACK #16 (RHYTHM SECTION ONLY)

COUNT OFF: 2 BARS (6 CLICKS)

School Street

GREG FISHMAN

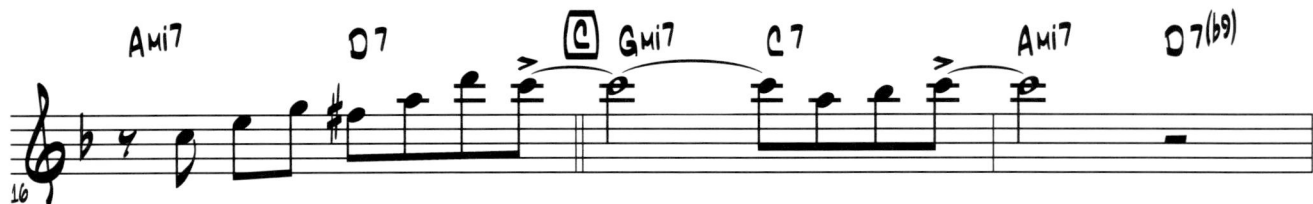

©2010 Greg Fishman Jazz Studios
All Rights Reserved. Copyright Secured.

CD TRACK #17 (SAXOPHONE + RHYTHM SECTION)
CD TRACK #18 (RHYTHM SECTION ONLY)

COUNT OFF: 2 BARS (6 CLICKS)

Greg Fishman

Lexington Avenue

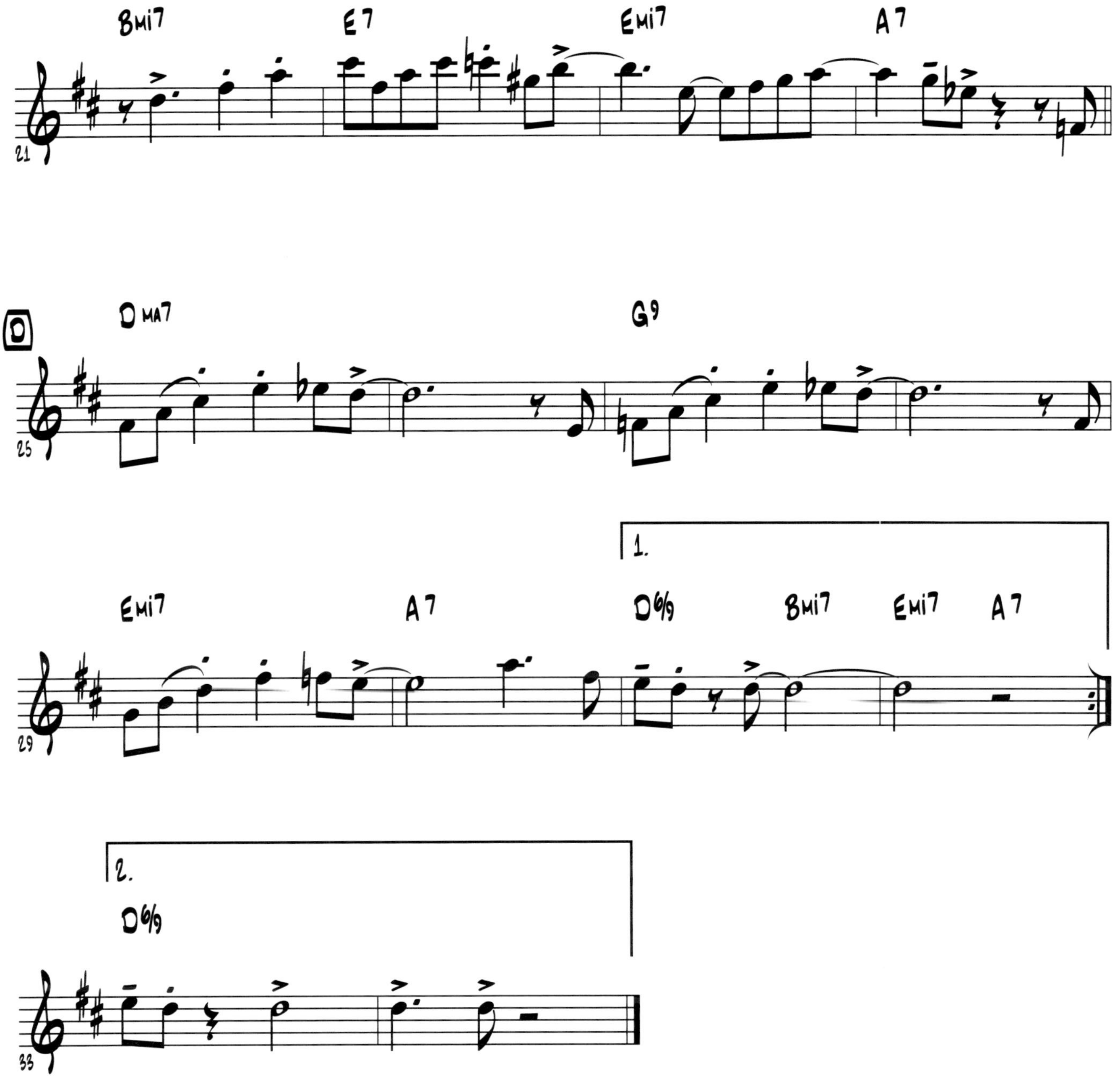
BMI7
E7
EMI7
A7
21
D
D MA7
G9
25
1.
EMI7
A7
D6/9
BMI7
EMI7
A7
29
2.
D6/9
33

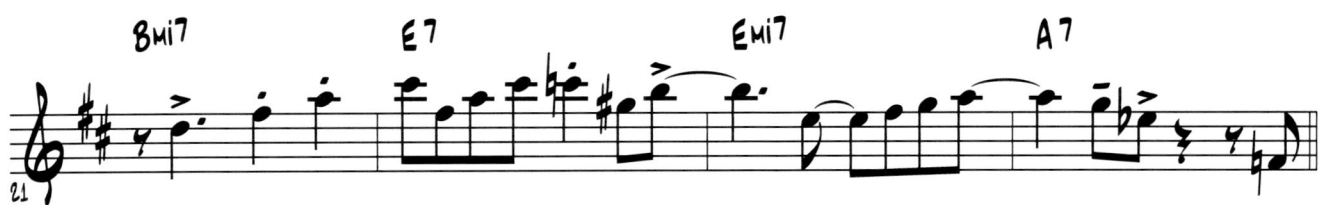

CD TRACK #19 (SAXOPHONE + RHYTHM SECTION)
CD TRACK #20 (RHYTHM SECTION ONLY)

COUNT OFF: 2 BARS (6 CLICKS)

Greg Fishman

Edgewater Avenue

THEMATIC INDEX

32

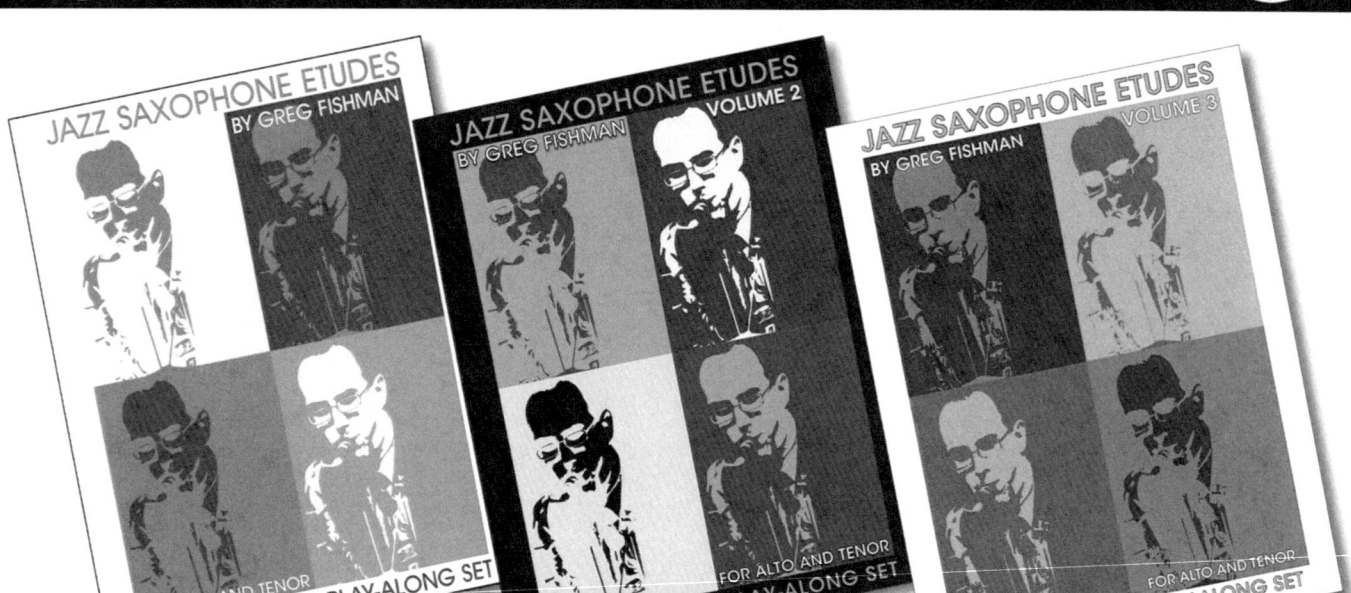

About the Author

Saxophonist and flutist Greg Fishman is an accomplished performer, recording artist, author, teacher and clinician. Born in Chicago in 1967, he began playing professionally at age fourteen. Greg graduated from DePaul University in Chicago with a degree in Jazz Performance, and earned a Masters Degree in Jazz Pedagogy from Northwestern University. He is among the foremost experts on the music of Stan Getz and is the author of three Getz transcription books published by Hal Leonard. His self-published books, *Jazz Saxophone Etudes, Volumes 1 – 3, Jazz Saxophone Duets, Volumes 1 – 3, Jazz Phrasing for Saxophone, Volumes 1 – 3, Jazz Guitar Etudes, Jazz Trumpet Duets* and *Tasting Harmony*™ are in circulation worldwide and have been endorsed by top educators and jazz performers, including Michael Brecker, Jerry Coker, Bob Sheppard, James Moody and Phil Woods.

Greg is a contributing author of jazz theory articles for Jazz Improv magazine, JAZZed, Chicago Jazz Magazine, IAJE Jazz Educators Journal, and was featured on the cover of *Saxophone Journal*, for whom he also writes. He is the author of the liner notes for the Verve reissue of the Getz recording *The Steamer*.

Greg has toured and performed worldwide with his own group, and with such artists as the Woody Herman Band, Louis Bellson, Slide Hampton, Conte Candoli, Lou Levy, Clark Terry, Jackie and Roy, Don Menza, Ira Sullivan, Judy Roberts, Jeremy Monteiro, Jimmy Heath, Lou Donaldson, Harry Allen, Jeff Hamilton, Eddie Higgins, and Benny Golson.

Greg is the co-founder, along with Brazilian guitarist/vocalist, Paulinho Garcia, of the award-winning duo, "Two for Brazil." They perform worldwide, and have recorded five CDs. Greg's current discography features additional jazz releases in the U.S., Singapore, and Japan.

In addition to clubs and concerts in the U.S., Greg has been featured at the Concord-Fujitsu jazz festival in Japan, the NorthSea Jazz Festival in the Netherlands, and in numerous concerts in Hong Kong, Bangkok, Singapore, China and Israel.

Greg teaches jazz master classes and college workshops nationally and internationally, and is on the faculty of the Jamey Aebersold Summer Jazz Workshop.

When not on tour, Greg is based in the Chicago area where he performs locally and teaches at Greg Fishman Jazz Studios.

Greg Fishman is a Rico artist and plays Rico reeds exclusively.

"...His solos are shrewdly conceived yet delivered with apparent ease and elegance. He develops harmonies that sometimes startle the ear as he forges lines that take unexpected twists and turns..."
— Chicago Tribune

"Greg Fishman dares to explore new musical heights. Every lesson in Greg's books is a must for all musicians, and this latest book is no exception. Greg, you've done a beautiful, musical thing again!"
— James Moody

The Acclaimed Jazz Learning Series from Greg Fishman
Jazz Saxophone Duets, Volumes 1-3

Jazz Saxophone Duets:
"Finally a hip jazz duet book from a sax man who can really play. I recommend this to any teacher who wants to share good music with his students." — Phil Woods

"I have known Greg Fishman for a long time. He has a very analytical mind. He knows how to get in between the cracks to give you what you need musically. *Jazz Saxophone Duets* is a good example of some of what he does."
— James Moody

"Perfect for the player who wants to improve his ear, technique and style. The duets are fresh, articulate and melodic enough to memorize."
— Plas Johnson

"This is a really fantastic book. Concise and practical, the duets are also melodic and extremely musical. What makes this book stand out is that it hits all of the basics necessary for the development of the skills essential to saxophonists of every level. It's a "must-have" for teachers as well as students. If you need a modern and musical duet book, *Jazz Saxophone Duets* reigns supreme!"
— Tim Price

"A post-bebop encyclopedia of sounds and melodic shapes that are required repertoire for any young jazz saxophonist."
— Dr. David Demsey, Professor of Music, William Paterson University

To order by phone or mail, contact:

**PM Woodwind
822 Custer Ave
Evanston, IL 60202
(847) 869-7049**

About the Author

Saxophonist and flutist Greg Fishman is an accomplished performer, recording artist, author, teacher and clinician. Born in Chicago in 1967, he began playing professionally at age fourteen. Greg graduated from DePaul University in Chicago with a degree in Jazz Performance, and earned a Masters Degree in Jazz Pedagogy from Northwestern University. He is among the foremost experts on the music of Stan Getz and is the author of three Getz transcription books published by Hal Leonard. His self-published books, *Jazz Saxophone Etudes, Volumes 1 – 3, Jazz Saxophone Duets, Volumes 1 – 3, Jazz Phrasing for Saxophone, Volumes 1 – 3, Jazz Guitar Etudes, Jazz Trumpet Duets* and *Tasting Harmony*™ are in circulation worldwide and have been endorsed by top educators and jazz performers, including Michael Brecker, Jerry Coker, Bob Sheppard, James Moody and Phil Woods.

Greg is a contributing author of jazz theory articles for Jazz Improv magazine, JAZZed, Chicago Jazz Magazine, IAJE Jazz Educators Journal, and was featured on the cover of *Saxophone Journal*, for whom he also writes. He is the author of the liner notes for the Verve reissue of the Getz recording *The Steamer*.

Greg has toured and performed worldwide with his own group, and with such artists as the Woody Herman Band, Louis Bellson, Slide Hampton, Conte Candoli, Lou Levy, Clark Terry, Jackie and Roy, Don Menza, Ira Sullivan, Judy Roberts, Jeremy Monteiro, Jimmy Heath, Lou Donaldson, Harry Allen, Jeff Hamilton, Eddie Higgins, and Benny Golson.

Greg is the co-founder, along with Brazilian guitarist/vocalist, Paulinho Garcia, of the award-winning duo, "Two for Brazil." They perform worldwide, and have recorded five CDs. Greg's current discography features additional jazz releases in the U.S., Singapore, and Japan.

In addition to clubs and concerts in the U.S., Greg has been featured at the Concord-Fujitsu jazz festival in Japan, the NorthSea Jazz Festival in the Netherlands, and in numerous concerts in Hong Kong, Bangkok, Singapore, China and Israel.

Greg teaches jazz master classes and college workshops nationally and internationally, and is on the faculty of the Jamey Aebersold Summer Jazz Workshop.

When not on tour, Greg is based in the Chicago area where he performs locally and teaches at Greg Fishman Jazz Studios.

Greg Fishman is a Rico artist and plays Rico reeds exclusively.

"...His solos are shrewdly conceived yet delivered with apparent ease and elegance. He develops harmonies that sometimes startle the ear as he forges lines that take unexpected twists and turns..."
— Chicago Tribune

"Greg Fishman dares to explore new musical heights. Every lesson in Greg's books is a must for all musicians, and this latest book is no exception. Greg, you've done a beautiful, musical thing again!"
— James Moody

Farm Animals to Spot

Illustrated by
Stephanie Fizer Coleman

Designed by Jenny Addison
Words by Kate Nolan

You can use the stickers to fill in the chart
at the back of the book, so you can keep
track of the animals you have seen.

Farmyard

Can be as tall as a young child

Embden goose
A big, heavy goose with pure white feathers and an orange beak. Listen out for its loud, honking call.

This is a male (cockerel)

Rhode Island Red chicken
Look for their reddish-brown feathers and bright red combs (crests) on their heads. Females (hens) lay light brown eggs.

This is a female (hen)

White Leghorn chicken
Spot its fan of snowy tail feathers and its short yellow beak. Hens lay large, white eggs.